T0061976

Minecraft Dungeons:

Gear

21st Century Skills **INNOVATION LIBRARY**

Josh Gregory

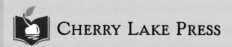

CHERRY LAKE PRESS

Published in the United States of America by Cherry Lake Publishing Group
Ann Arbor, Michigan
www.cherrylakepublishing.com

Reading Adviser: Beth Walker Gambro, MS, Ed., Reading Consultant, Yorkville, IL

Cherry Lake Press is an imprint of Cherry Lake Publishing Group.

Library of Congress Cataloging-in-Publication Data has been filed and is available at catalog.loc.gov

Cherry Lake Publishing Group would like to acknowledge the work of the Partnership for 21st Century Learning, a Network of Battelle for Kids. Please visit http://www.battelleforkids.org/networks/p21 for more information.

Printed in the United States of America
Corporate Graphics

Josh Gregory is the author of more than 200 books for kids. He has written about everything from animals to technology to history. A graduate of the University of Missouri–Columbia, he currently lives in Chicago, Illinois.

Contents

CHAPTER 1

Dressed for the Dungeon

If you've spent a lot of time playing *Minecraft*, you've probably **crafted** more than a few swords and sets of armor. This gear makes it a lot easier to explore *Minecraft*'s more dangerous areas and defeat the enemies that lurk within. But equipping new gear in *Minecraft* doesn't change much about the way combat actually works. The very best sword in the game works the same way as the most basic one. It's just stronger.

If you've ever wanted a bigger variety of gear or more complex combat in *Minecraft*, *Minecraft Dungeons* might be the game for you. Released in 2020, it is a dungeon crawler game set in the world of *Minecraft*. In dungeon crawlers, the main goal is to keep improving your character so you can defeat tougher and tougher enemies. And in *Minecraft Dungeons*, the main way to improve your character is to seek out new gear.

You'll find all kinds of useful things to equip on your character in *Minecraft Dungeons*, from weapons to armor and much more. Almost every one of these items will change your character in big ways. Your attacks will change. You will receive different special abilities to help turn the tide in battle. You will be able to withstand different amounts of damage from enemy attacks. These differences can be extremely drastic. Playing with one set of gear might almost feel like a completely different game than playing with another set.

You can check out a close-up view of your character wearing their gear each time you start the game.

Adventuring in Style

Not everything you find in *Minecraft Dungeons* is there to make your character stronger or give you new abilities. Some items are just for looks! For example, there are a number of capes you can equip on your character. You can also equip a pet that will follow your character around. These pets do not attack enemies or offer any advantage. They just look cool.

You won't earn these kinds of cosmetic items by defeating enemies or opening chests. Many of them come from purchasing downloadable content (DLC) packs. Others can be earned by participating in special limited-time events in the game. If you ever see a friend with an interesting cape or pet, try asking them how they got it!

As you gather more and more gear in *Minecraft Dungeons*, you'll get used to spending a lot of time in the game's **inventory** screen. This is where you can look at everything you have and check out the details of each piece of gear. You can also organize everything you have and change what you have equipped on your character.

Be careful any time you open your inventory. The game does not pause while you are looking at this screen. This means enemies can attack you while you are busy sorting through your items. If this happens, you'll hear the sounds of combat even though you can't see what's going on. Close your inventory and take care of the threat before you find yourself looking at the game over screen. Or, better yet, be sure to take care of any nearby threats and find a safe spot before you even open up the inventory.

Are you ready to dive in and start building your gear collection? There's a lot to learn at first. But once you have a handle on things, you'll be sifting through axes, armor, and much more in search of the very best gear the game has to offer.

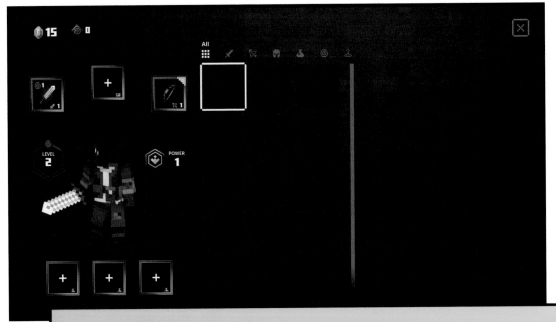

You'll start the game with a pretty empty inventory, but it is sure to fill up quickly.

CHAPTER 2

Types of Gear

Most of the gear you find in *Minecraft Dungeons* can be organized into four main categories. The first is armor. In most dungeon crawlers, you will find all kinds of different armor to mix and match. You might have separate slots to equip gloves, helmets, and body armor, for example. But in *Minecraft Dungeons*, armor is very simple. There is only one slot, and all armor comes as a full suit. Every time you equip a new set of armor, your character's appearance will change to show the new outfit. But armor is about a lot more than just looks.

Each piece of gear you equip gives you different benefits. With armor, these benefits almost always focus on allowing you to withstand enemy attacks. Sometimes this means the armor will give you additional health points. Other times, the armor will reduce the amount of damage you take from enemy attacks in the first place. Usually, a set of armor will offer a combination of these two things. Sometimes you will also find armor that adds other special bonuses as well. For example, you might find a set of armor that is especially strong against ice attacks. Or you might find another set that makes your character run faster. Different sets of armor will be useful in different situations, so it's good to keep a variety around.

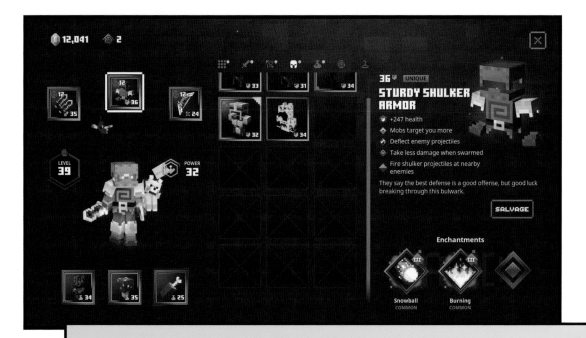

Armor allows your character to keep fighting even as you take damage from enemy attacks.

Not all melee weapons are as basic as swords and axes. You might even find yourself wielding a knife made of shiny pink coral!

The next category of gear to look out for is **melee** weapons. A melee weapon is a weapon you can use up close in hand-to-hand combat. As with armor, you can only equip one at a time. Melee weapons come in all kinds of different forms, from swords and axes to daggers and hammers. Each type of weapon handles a bit differently in combat. For example, daggers can be swung very quickly, but each hit typically does only a little damage. They also require you to be very, very close to an enemy for attacks to land. On the other hand, a long, slow weapon like a glaive does more damage with each hit and has greater range. Which types of weapons you like to use best is something you can only learn by experimenting. Give each type a try and see what feels good for your play style.

Of course, each melee weapon also has stats to consider. The main one is damage. Each time you hit an enemy with a melee weapon, it will do a random

The Perfect Pet

Some artifacts will give you the ability to call a pet to follow you around on your adventures. This kind of pet is much different from the ones you can equip as cosmetic items. A pet from an artifact can give you a huge advantage in combat as you make your way through the game's most dangerous environments. These powerful creatures can attack enemies and do quite a bit of damage. Perhaps even more importantly, they can distract enemies from attacking your character. This leaves you free to launch your own attacks while your pet keeps the monsters busy.

Eventually, your pet will probably take enough damage to be defeated. Don't worry, though. After some time passes, you will be able to summon them once again.

amount of damage within a certain range of numbers. For example, one weapon might have a damage range of 22 to 38. Another might do between 30 and 40 damage per hit. Higher numbers are always better here. But you should also consider the attack speed of a weapon. For example, you might have a dagger that does just slightly less damage per hit than a hammer. Overall, the dagger can probably still do more damage than the hammer because it takes less time between swings.

With a ranged weapon like this, each hit only does 50 damage. However, each time you fire, the weapon will hit two times. This means the actual damage is 100.

Just as with armor, each melee weapon can also have other special traits that set it apart. For example, you might find a weapon that does extra damage against certain types of enemies. Or you might find one that makes enemies move slower for a while after you hit them. Keep different weapons with special abilities in your inventory to help you against specific enemy types.

Your melee weapon isn't the only way to deal damage in *Minecraft Dungeons*. You also have a slot where you can equip a ranged weapon. This is a weapon that lets you attack from a distance. These are usually bows or crossbows. Just like melee weapons, each one does damage within a certain range of numbers. But there are other things to consider as well. For example, some ranged weapons fire multiple shots at once. Others have shots that can pass through enemies to strike others behind them. Even when the damage numbers are lower, these weapons might be able to do more overall damage.

The fourth category of gear is made up of artifacts. These are special items that each give your character a special ability to use in combat. You can equip up to three of them at a time. The abilities you get from artifacts vary widely. Some give you special healing spells. Others give you a burst of speed. Some are attacks that can cause huge damage to enemies. Other can be used to simply push enemies away in case you get swarmed. Each time you use an artifact ability, you will have to wait a few seconds before you can use it again. This is called a cooldown timer.

Armor, melee weapons, and ranged weapons can be further improved using enchantments. Enchantments

Some artifact abilities let you do huge damage to enemies. These are especially handy when fighting bosses.

An enchantment like poison cloud can quickly cut down huge groups of enemies.

are special traits that make an item even more powerful. For example, you might be able to enchant your armor so it does damage to any enemy that hits you. Or you might enchant your melee weapon so it heals your character each time you hit an enemy.

Each piece of gear can have anywhere from one to three enchantment slots. In each slot, you will get to choose between two or three enchantments. You can

At its highest level, or tier, an enchantment can be extremely powerful.

only choose one per slot, and the possible choices are random. You'll unlock them using enchantment points. These are earned each time you level up your character, which is done by defeating enemies.

Each enchantment also has multiple levels. For example, choosing the first level of an enchantment might cost one enchantment point and give you a 10 percent damage boost. Choosing the second level could cost two more enchantment points and give you a 20 percent boost. And finally, the third level might cost an additional three points and give you a 30 percent boost.

Better gear will give you more enchantment options. It will also offer stronger enchantments than the gear you find early on in the game. So if the enchantments you're finding aren't that exciting, just keep searching. You'll find better things as you keep playing!

The first level of an enchantment typically only costs one enchantment point.

CHAPTER 3

The Thrill of the Search

Seeking out new gear for your character is a big part of the fun in any dungeon crawler. *Minecraft Dungeons* is no exception. Once you finish the game's main storyline, most of your time will be spent building up your character and looking for better and better gear. But where should you look to find just the right items? And how do you know when you've found something truly special?

As you move through dungeons, don't stop too long to think before picking up a piece of gear. You should have plenty of space in your inventory, and even items you don't need still have something to offer. When you are in your inventory screen, select an item you don't want. Then choose "salvage." This option will destroy the item and give you some emeralds, which work as money in *Minecraft Dungeons*. If you invested any enchantment points in an item, you will also get those back. This means there is no downside to picking up gear and spending your enchantment points freely!

After each mission, you will return to camp. This is the perfect time to look through your inventory and see what you've picked up recently. No enemies will bother you, and you can take your time. Check to see if anything you picked up is better than your current

You should consider salvaging every item you don't plan on using in the near future.

gear. Compare stats and look to see if anything has enchantment options that seem interesting.

You might notice that some items have a white background, while others are green or orange. White items are the most common kind. They are less likely to have the best stats, though they can still be quite powerful. Green items are rare. They are slightly more likely than common items to have powerful stats and

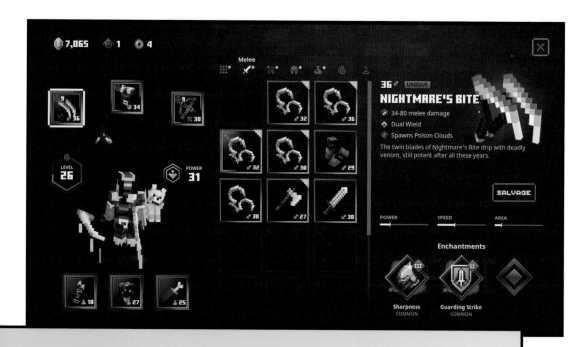

It's always thrilling to discover a powerful, new, unique item.

abilities. Finally, orange items are unique gear. These are typically some of the best items you will find. Your chances of finding rare and unique items are lower than your chances of finding common items.

Each item also has a number in the bottom right corner of its box. This is its level. This is a good way of getting a quick idea of how powerful a piece of gear is. Higher numbers typically mean a stronger piece of gear. Be careful, though. Sometimes an item with a lower level will be more effective than one with a higher level because of its abilities. Be sure to think carefully about what you need from your gear.

Are you looking for a certain type of weapon or armor? When you are on the Mission Select screen, choose a dungeon. Some information will pop up. At the bottom of this box, you will see which kinds of items are found in the dungeon. This does not guarantee you will find those items every time you play the dungeon. However, it does tell you which dungeons you need to play if you want a chance at getting the item you want. The difficulty level you choose when selecting a mission will also affect which gear you find. Higher difficulty levels give you access to gear with higher levels.

Once you're in a dungeon, there are a few different ways to find items. The simplest is to just defeat enemies. As you do, some of them will drop gear on the ground. All you need to do is pick it up. A lot of great gear is also hidden throughout the world. If you just speed from the beginning of a mission to the end, you'll probably miss a lot of it. Instead, take your time and try to find all of the secrets in each dungeon. Start by opening up your map screen. This will show you where you have explored and where you still need to go. It will also tell you how many treasure chests and secrets are remaining in the mission. This is very helpful

Treasure Pigs

Sometimes as you are exploring the world of *Minecraft Dungeons*, you might come across a strange-looking creature that tries to run away from you. If you look closely, you'll see that it's a pig with a treasure chest strapped to its back. Usually, these pigs will show up in the middle of a group of enemies that you need to take care of. But do your best to take out the treasure pig as well so you can get the gear it's carrying. This can be tricky, as the pig will dart all over the place trying to avoid your attacks. The rewards are worth the trouble, though.

when you're trying to figure out if you've found everything. Be sure to explore areas that are off the beaten path. If the game's main mission is telling you to go in one direction, the other direction almost always holds some kind of treasure!

You can also seek out new gear by talking to the various merchants in your camp. To get access to these

You'll usually find the very strongest gear by defeating enemies, but merchants often have strong items for sale too.

merchants, you'll first need to find and rescue them from the game's dungeons. Each merchant offers a different range of gear. For example, the luxury merchant sells high-quality items, but they are fairly expensive. The village merchant has lower prices, but their items are usually not as powerful. The mystery

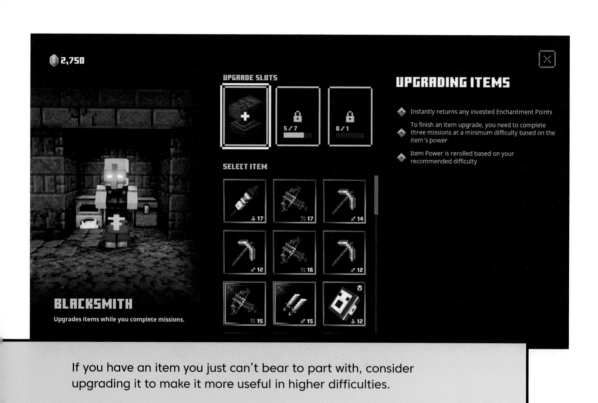

UPGRADE SLOTS

5 / 7

0 / 1

UPGRADING ITEMS

Instantly returns any invested Enchantment Points

To finish an item upgrade, you need to complete three missions at a minimum difficulty based on the item's power

Item Power is rerolled based on your recommended difficulty

SELECT ITEM

17   17   14

12   16   12

15   15   12

BLACKSMITH
Upgrades items while you complete missions.

2,750

If you have an item you just can't bear to part with, consider upgrading it to make it more useful in higher difficulties.

merchant sells all kinds of items, but you won't know what you're getting until you buy it. The blacksmith does not sell you new gear at all. Instead, you can give him things you already own and he will make them stronger. This is very useful if you have a weapon you like to use, but you've reached a point in the game where it doesn't do enough damage.

If you've been playing *Minecraft Dungeons* long enough, you might start to get tired of seeing some of the same gear over and over again. If this happens, consider trying out some of the game's downloadable content (DLC). Each DLC pack costs a few dollars and offers new levels, enemies, and types of gear to find. Players with all the DLC packs will have access to a lot of gear that isn't available in the main game.

CHAPTER 4

The Best Builds

Different combinations of gear can make a huge difference in how you approach fights in *Minecraft Dungeons*. One set of gear might make your character perfect for storming into big groups of enemies and absorbing tons of damage. Another might be better for attacking from a distance and avoiding damage altogether.

The set of gear you have equipped in *Minecraft Dungeons* is called your build. The most dedicated players will plan and tweak every possible detail of a build. This allows them to make their characters as strong as possible. You probably don't need to go too in-depth to enjoy the game or finish the main story. But if you want to really create an effective character, you'll need to do at least some planning with your build.

The main thing to think about is how your weapons, armor, and artifacts will work together. Many enchantments and artifact abilities are able to give each other bonuses. For example, an enchantment on your weapon might make pets summoned by artifacts more powerful than normal. Or an armor enchantment

An enchantment like this can greatly increase the potency of your pets.

might make healing abilities stronger. Think carefully about each item you equip and how it will fit with the rest of your gear.

In many dungeon crawlers, putting together a build is a process that lasts throughout the entire game. You

Tired of the gear you've got? Pick up some emerald-finding gear and start saving up to buy new stuff from the merchants.

A little green arrow means a piece of gear is stronger than the one you are currently using.

often need to commit to decisions about which kind of character you want to create from the very beginning. These choices might even be permanent, locking you into a specific play style unless you create a new character. But in *Minecraft Dungeons*, the only thing you need to think about is your gear. This means you can completely change your character's build at any point. All you need to do is equip a new set of gear.

You can even keep multiple sets of gear in your inventory and switch builds to fit different situations. It's a very flexible system, so feel free to experiment.

One situation where you might want to try different builds is in multiplayer. When playing with friends, it's best to make sure each player plays a specific role. For example, one person might be the "tank" who draws

Testing Things Out

Want to see just how much damage your build is able to do? When you're in camp, go to the right of the main square area. Here you'll find a couple of scarecrows. You can attack them just like enemies. They won't hit back, but you'll see damage numbers pop up above them when you hit them. This tells you just how much damage you are doing with your attacks. It's a great way to make sure your build is working before diving into a more dangerous situation.

RECYCLER

Being hit by damage-inflicting projectiles will occasionally craft a small quiver of arrows.

UPGRADE TIERS

I Every 30th projectile

II Every 20th projectile

III Every 10th projectile

UPGRADE 1

31 COMMON

SPROUT ARMOR

+177 health

Health potions heal nearby allies

Traps and poisons nearby mobs when rolling

The dark vines of the Sprout Armor continue to grow even in complete darkness.

SALVAGE

Enchantments

Empty Slot   Recycler
COMMON

An enchantment like this would be extremely useful for a build focusing on ranged attacks.

enemies' attention. Another might focus on healing, while a third uses ranged weapons and artifacts to do damage. Try out different build combinations and strategies to see what works!

GLOSSARY

cosmetic (kahz-MEH-tik) relating to how something looks

crafted (KRAF-tid) made or built something

inventory (IN-vuhn-toh-ree) a list of the items your character is carrying in a video game

melee (MAY-lay) relating to hand-to-hand combat

FIND OUT MORE

Books

Milton, Stephanie. *Guide to Minecraft Dungeons: A Handbook for Heroes*. New York: Del Rey, 2020.

Zeiger, Jennifer. *The Making of Minecraft*. Ann Arbor, MI: Cherry Lake Publishing, 2017.

Websites

Minecraft Dungeons
https://www.minecraft.net/en-us/about-dungeons
Check out the official *Minecraft Dungeons* website for the latest updates on the game.

Minecraft Dungeons Wiki
https://minecraft.fandom.com/wiki/Minecraft_Dungeons
This fan-created wiki is packed with useful details about *Minecraft Dungeons* and its DLC.

INDEX